For Peter
—A.P.

In memory of Mariann,
intrepid traveler, great neighbor,
and kind friend
—M.S.

THIS IS A BORZOI BOOK PUBLISHED BY ALFRED A. KNOPF

Text copyright © 2012 by Alicia Potter
Jacket art and interior illustrations copyright © 2012 by Melissa Sweet
Jacket and interior photographs courtesy of Mary Lobisco

All rights reserved. Published in the United States by Alfred A. Knopf,
an imprint of Random House Children's Books, a division of Random
House, Inc., New York.

Knopf, Borzoi Books, and the colophon are registered trademarks of
Random House, Inc.

Visit us on the Web! randomhouse.com/kids

Educators and librarians, for a variety of teaching tools, visit
us at randomhouse.com/teachers

Library of Congress Cataloging-in-Publication Data
Potter, Alicia.
Mrs. Harkness and the panda / by Alicia Potter ; illustrated
by Melissa Sweet. — 1st edition.
p.   cm.
ISBN 978-0-375-84448-5 (trade) —
ISBN 978-0-375-94448-2 (lib. bdg.)
1. Giant panda. 2. Wild animal collecting—China. 3. Harkness,
Ruth. I. Sweet, Melissa, ill. II. Title.
QL737.C27P648 2011
599.789—dc22
2010025287

The text of this book is set in 14-point Bernhard Modern BT.
The illustrations were created using watercolor and mixed media.

MANUFACTURED IN CHINA
March 2012
10 9 8 7 6 5 4 3 2 1

First Edition

MRS. HARKNESS
AND THE PANDA

written by
ALICIA POTTER

illustrated by
MELISSA SWEET

Alfred A. Knopf   New York

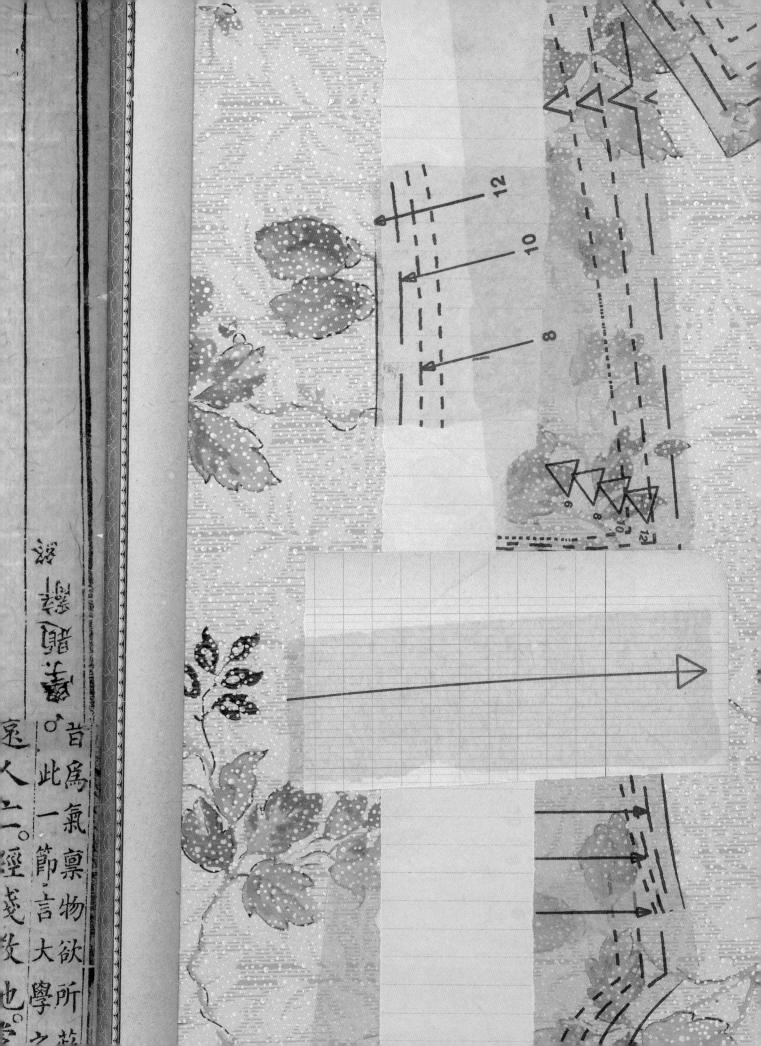

譯標譜書。此一節言大學之

首鳥氣稟物欲所蔽

遠人二。經矣。……也。

In 1934, Ruth Harkness had never seen a panda bear.
Not many people in the world had.

Pandas were shy and lived in the mountains of China. The terrain was so wild, so treacherous, that few explorers dared to risk it. But Mrs. Harkness knew one who was brave enough.

Her husband. On September 22, 1934, William Harkness set off to bring the first live panda to the United States.

Soon the whole world would know the panda!

Mrs. Harkness wanted to go with him. But women were considered too dainty for exploring. Still, she hoped to join Mr. Harkness at the end of his expedition. An adventure together!

Many months passed. Then, on a winter afternoon, Mrs. Harkness received terrible news. Her husband had died in China. Mrs. Harkness was very sad. She had loved him so.

That love inspired her to carry on with his work.

Mrs. Harkness would go to China. She would find the panda.

"I had inherited an expedition," she said.

Mrs. Harkness lived in New York City. She designed tea gowns. She wasn't particularly strong, athletic, or daring. And except for her cats, Tibby and Baggy, she knew little about animals.

But she did know that bringing back a panda would be hard. Impossible, even.

"One chance in a million," she said.

Mrs. Harkness's friends scoffed.

"You're no explorer!"

"You're out of your head!"

"Don't forget, your husband died trying to find the panda!"

Mrs. Harkness didn't listen. She *knew* her husband had died trying to find the panda. And now she had an expedition to plan.

On April 17, 1936, Mrs. Harkness set off on a steamer for China.
Her ship sailed the Red Sea . . .

. . . through ports in Ceylon . . .

Ceylon

Lake and Boat-House. - Nuwara-Eliya.

SIX CENTS

. . . and Singapore . . .

Fishing Canoe with outrigger.
Colombo.

. . . and then finally China!

41. HARBOR OF HONG KONG, CHINA.

Mrs. Harkness arrived in Hong Kong, with its hidden coves and rocky islands and a harbor a-bob with sailboats called junks.

When a little girl waved three times, Mrs. Harkness took it as a sign of good luck.

Her next stop was Shanghai, where she met a friend of her husband's. He scoffed.

But Mrs. Harkness didn't listen.
She had an expedition to continue.

Finally, she met one person who didn't think she was crazy. He was a dashing young man named Yang Di Lin, or, as he was called in English, Quentin Young. Quentin knew the bamboo forests. He had seen pandas. He decided to help Mrs. Harkness.

First, she had to have the right clothes. Explorer's clothes. A tailor cut Mr. Harkness's clothes to fit Mrs. Harkness: a fur-hooded parka, woolen underwear, riding trousers, slacks, shirts, and an old tweed jacket.

Packing List
shirts
scarfs
socks
sweaters

tailor Bill's tweed coat

cut Bill's boots
to fit

Next a shoemaker cobbled down a pair of Mr. Harkness's bulky boots to fit Mrs. Harkness's little feet. "They probably had two pounds of nails apiece," declared Mrs. Harkness.

Then she and Quentin packed. And packed. And packed. They packed maps and sleeping bags, medicine and rope, wire and flea powder. They packed guns for protection. Mrs. Harkness even packed a bottle and dried milk, just in case the panda was a baby. They packed twenty-two pieces of luggage!

Late at night on September 26, Mrs. Harkness and Quentin set off to find their panda.
They sailed for two weeks up the golden Yangtze River.

YELLOW
SEA

SHANGHAI

HONG KONG

TAIWAN

SOUTH CHINA
SEA

They reached Chungking and then drove three hundred miles—past rice paddies and water buffalo and tiny hillside farms—to Chengdu.

Mrs. Harkness hired a jolly, fat cook named Wang. She hired sixteen men to carry the twenty-two pieces of luggage. She kept on moving.

Although not always on her own two feet. Sometimes Mrs. Harkness rode on a contraption called a *wha-gar*.

But she did some walking. When the heavy boots blistered her feet, she traded them for rope sandals like the ones the Chinese men wore.

The journey was so rough that Mrs. Harkness almost cried. Still, she didn't turn back. She had an expedition to finish.

Near a ruined Buddhist temple, the expedition met an old man with wild gray hair and no teeth named Lao Tsang. He told Mrs. Harkness and Quentin that he knew where to find *"bei-shung"*—the Chinese word for "panda." He would take them there.

In one day, they climbed, scrambled, and stumbled for nearly thirty miles.

They pitched camp. High in the mountains, the men set traps to capture the panda alive.

They found panda droppings. But no pandas.
They discovered bamboo stalks that pandas had crunched. But no pandas.
They saw claw marks on trees. But no pandas.

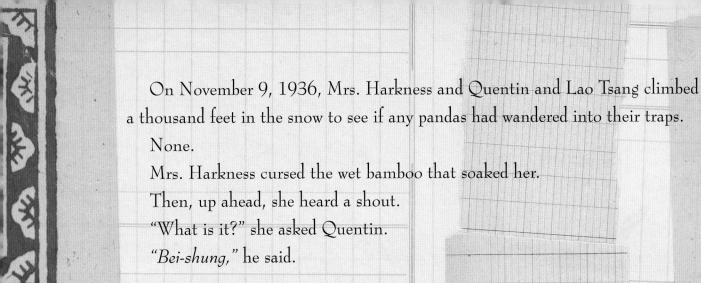

On November 9, 1936, Mrs. Harkness and Quentin and Lao Tsang climbed a thousand feet in the snow to see if any pandas had wandered into their traps.

None.

Mrs. Harkness cursed the wet bamboo that soaked her.

Then, up ahead, she heard a shout.

"What is it?" she asked Quentin.

"*Bei-shung,*" he said.

Mrs. Harkness struggled after Quentin through the damp branches. Quentin stopped at an old dead tree. From the tree came a whimper. *"Mwaaaa."*

A baby panda!

Quentin tucked the baby in his shirt, and he and Mrs. Harkness slid and staggered back to camp. Good thing Mrs. Harkness had packed that baby bottle!

Mrs. Harkness named the wriggly, furry bundle Su Lin. It means "a little bit of something very cute."

Mrs. Harkness had accomplished her husband's mission! *Their* mission. She hastened to return to America. But first she had two very important things to do.

She scattered her husband's ashes in the Chinese mountains.

And she thanked Quentin, her guide and friend, who had made the dangerous but exhilarating expedition possible. She gave him a carved gold ring to give to his fiancée. It was her wedding band.

News of Su Lin spread fast. When Mrs. Harkness arrived in America with the panda in her arms, reporters were waiting for her. *"Panda-monium!"* roared the headlines.

None of these newspaper stories called Mrs. Harkness crazy.

Or foolish.

Or reckless.

Su Lin, Panda Baby, Checks In at the Biltmore

NEW YORK TIMES, DECEMBER 24, 1936

BABY PANDA HE[R]
ENJOYS ITS BOTT[LE]

Panda-monium!

They called her a "woman explorer."

BOSTON POST, DECEMBER 24, 1936

BABY GIANT PANDA ARRIVES:
Mrs. Harkness' Specimen Only One in Captivity

SAN FRANCISCO CHRONICLE   DECEMBER 19, 1936

Everything Is Fine 'n Danda!
S.F.'s Finally Got A Panda

Mrs. Harkness found Su Lin a home away from home in the Brookfield Zoo, just outside Chicago. Scientists rushed to study the cub. And everyone came to see it. No animal had ever received so much attention. Now the whole world knew the panda!

Mrs. Harkness, too, found a home away from home . . .

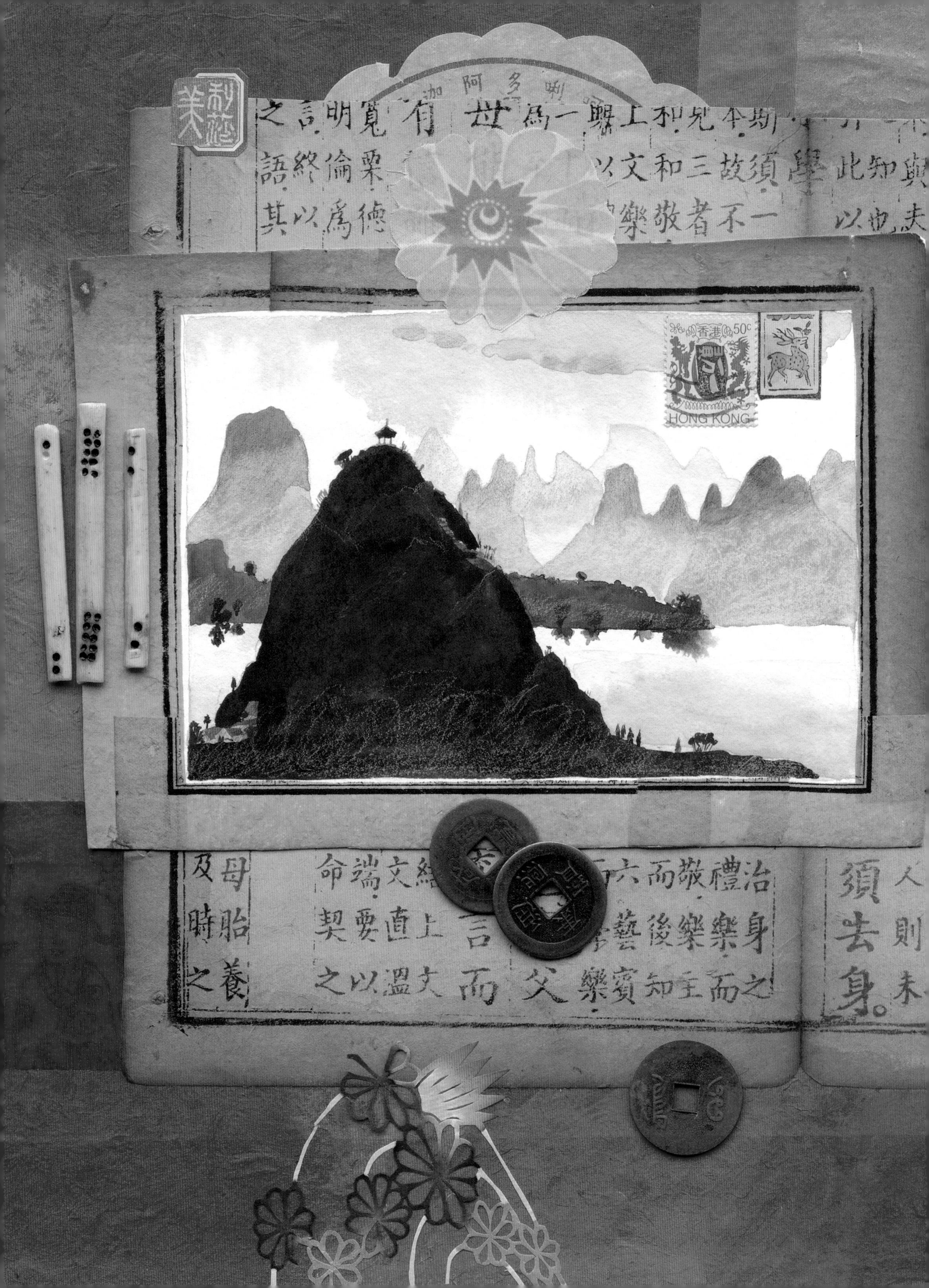
香港 50c
HONG KONG

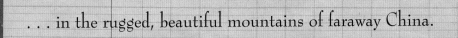

CHRONOLOGY OF
EVENTS

September 21, 1900—Ruth McCombs is born in Titusville, Pennsylvania.

September 9, 1934—She marries her friend of ten years, explorer William Harvest Harkness, Jr.

September 22, 1934—William Harkness leaves for China in search of the panda.

February 19, 1936—William Harkness dies of cancer while on expedition in China.

April 17, 1936—Ruth Harkness sets sail for China.

August 1936—In Shanghai, Harkness meets her guide, Quentin Young.

September 26, 1936—Harkness and Young leave Shanghai and begin their expedition.

November 9, 1936—Harkness and Young discover the baby panda Su Lin.

December 18, 1936—Harkness and Su Lin arrive in San Francisco.

February 1937—Su Lin finds a home in the Brookfield Zoo, just outside Chicago.

August 1937—The opening of Su Lin's exhibit attracts a record-setting crowd. It is a front-page story in the *Chicago Tribune* for nine days straight.

1938—Harkness publishes a memoir of her journey, *The Lady and the Panda*.

February 1938—After returning to China, Harkness brings back another panda, Mei-Mei, in the hope of mating it with Su Lin. Both pandas, however, turn out to be male.

April 1, 1938—Su Lin dies of pneumonia. (The panda is now a mounted exhibit at Chicago's Field Museum.)

July 19, 1947—Harkness dies at age forty-six.

Author's Note

Those patched eyes. That roly-poly body. The bold black-and-white fur. Who doesn't love a panda? Thank Ruth Harkness for that. Of course, today we might question whether it was right to take a baby panda from the wild. Our attitudes about animal conservation and zoos, as well as our knowledge of pandas' behavior, are much different than they were in the 1930s. Back then, before the advent of television and widespread commercial air travel, zoos were the primary way for people, including scientists, to learn about and appreciate animals—particularly rare or unusual species.

But even today, many conservationists admire Harkness's contribution to zoology. In bringing Su Lin to America, Harkness introduced the world to a tubby, bamboo-chomping ambassador. After Su Lin, the race to kill pandas for sport eventually lost much of its appeal. Instead, people rooted for their survival. Meanwhile, scientists, who once doubted that the bears existed (they were considered mythical beasts, like unicorns, even in China), began to study their biology and behavior.

In our time, the panda is so beloved that it is the symbol of the World Wildlife Fund, the international organization dedicated to saving the world's 2,500 giant pandas, as well as other endangered animals. On its website, the WWF credits Harkness and Su Lin with "evoking universal sympathy for the plight of the species." Indeed, we still feel wonder at the sight of these very cute creatures. Thousands of viewers visit Internet "panda cams" set up by zoos and sanctuaries, and in 2005 it was reminiscent of 1937 when crowds flocked to the National Zoo and San Diego Zoo to catch a glimpse of new panda cubs—one named, not so coincidentally, Su Lin.

Selected Bibliography

In addition to articles and online resources, these titles proved invaluable:

Croke, Vicki Constantine. *The Lady and the Panda.* New York: Random House, 2005.

Harkness, Ruth. *The Lady and the Panda.* New York: Carrick and Evans, 1938.

Kiefer, Michael. *Chasing the Panda.* New York: Four Walls Eight Windows, 2002.

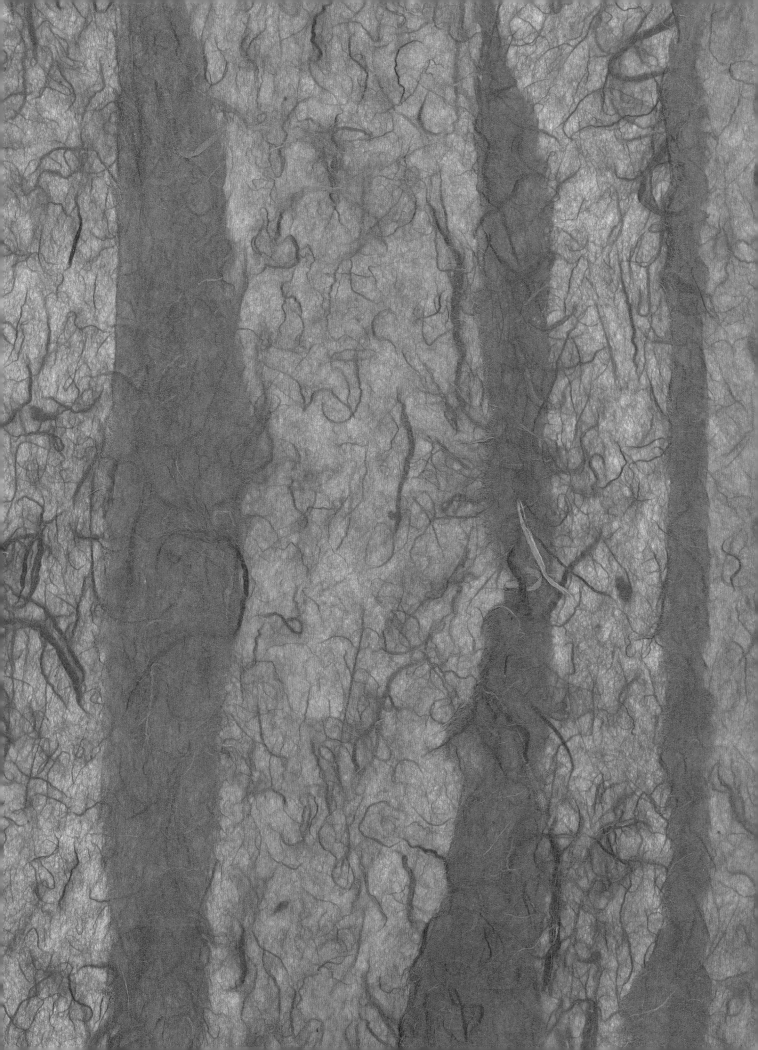